MW01274313

LAND OF CONTRASTS

Exploring the Peninsula Through Photographs and Writings

James E. Kuhn

with Poetic Insights by Dr. Vreneli E. Kuhn Wilson

The Boojum Tree arches its spine in grotesque beauty.

SUNSCAPE PUBLICATIONS
El Centro, California

Front cover: Sand Verbena near San Felipe
Preceding page: Boojum Trees at Cataviña
Back cover: Natural arch at Cabo San Lucas

Copyright © 1998 by James E. Kuhn

Cover and Interior Design by Curtis Boyer

Prepress by ColorType, San Diego, California

Map illustrations kindly provided by Norman C. Roberts

Printed in Hong Kong

Published by:
Sunscape Publications
1625 Drew Road
El Centro, California 92243

SUNSCAPE PUBLICATIONS

Kuhn, James E.
     Baja California : land of contrasts : exploring the peninsula
through photographs and writings / James E. Kuhn ; poetic insights
by Vreneli E. Kuhn Wilson. — 1st ed.
         p. cm.
     Includes bibliographical references.
     Preassigned LCCN: 97-91093
     ISBN: 0-9660889-0-5

     1. Baja California (Mexico) — Pictorial works. 2. Baja
California (Mexico) — Description and travel. 3. Baja California
(Mexico) — Poetry. 4. Natural history — Mexico — Baja California —
Pictorial works.   I. Wilson, Vreneli E. Kuhn. II. Title.

F1246.K84 1998   917.2′204′836
                                  QB197-41206

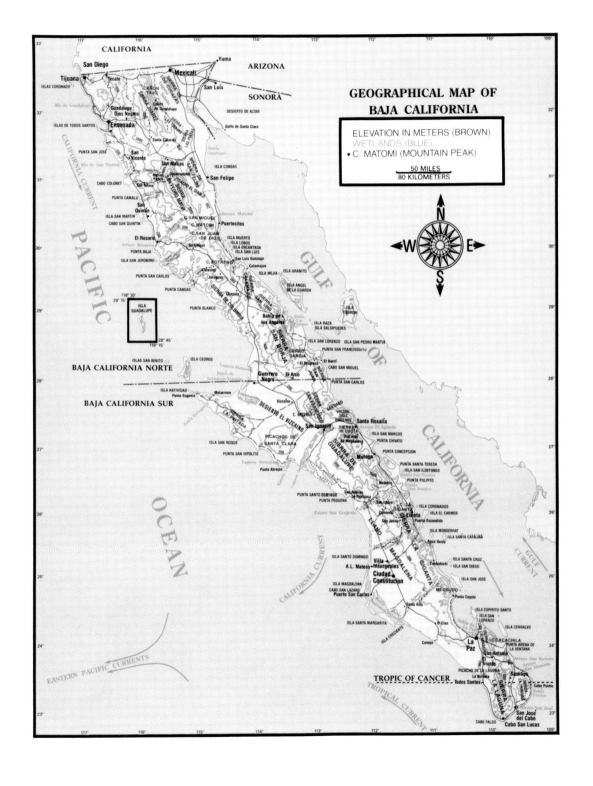

GEOGRAPHICAL MAP OF BAJA CALIFORNIA

ELEVATION IN METERS (BROWN)
WETLANDS (BLUE)
• C. MATOMI (MOUNTAIN PEAK)

50 MILES
80 KILOMETERS

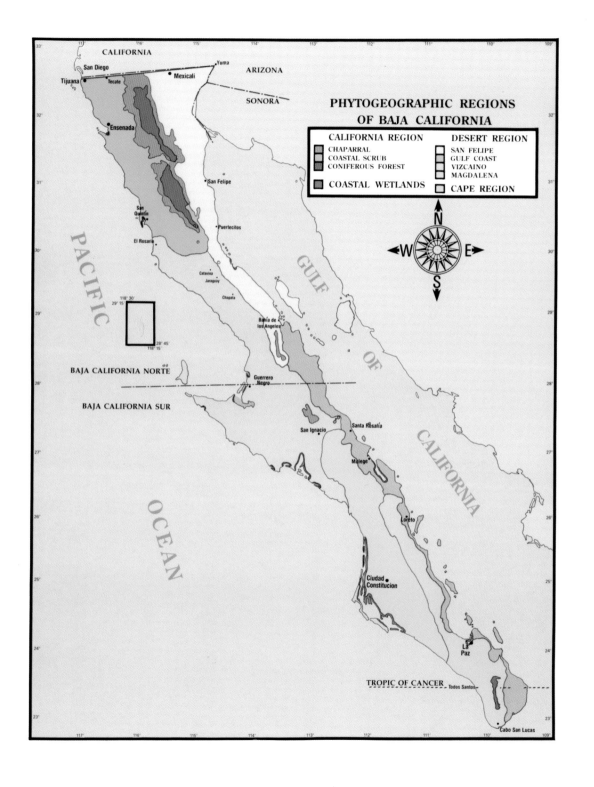

Contents

Introduction
9

Along the Sea of Cortez
12

Roaming the Interior Deserts & Canyons
24

Trekking the Sierras & Foothills
38

Exploring the Islands & Pacific Ocean
48

About the Authors
59

Selected Bibliography and Additional Reading
61

Acknowledgments
62

To the Kuhn and Wilson families for instilling in all of us a will to live every moment to the fullest and to learn something new every day. To Grandpa Kuhn for teaching us to "drive slow enough to see the lizards on the side of the road."

To my wife for her patience, love, support, knowledge, and, most of all, sharing these great times together!

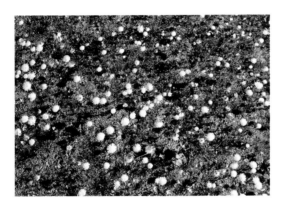

$\mathcal{I}$ntroduction

The magic of Mexico's Baja California peninsula lies in its contrasting landscapes. Reaching over 1,000 miles from its northern border with the United States to its tip at Cabo San Lucas, the peninsula is like no other on earth. This long strip of land narrows to distances less than 30 miles across, while reaching only 150 miles at its widest.

Though many assume the land to be a remote and waterless desert, conjuring images of cactus and *arroyos* (dry washes), few realize that its highest point is 10,154 feet, high enough to support alpine forests and annual snowfall. A mere 30 miles to the east of this peak, the land plunges to the Gulf of California (Sea of Cortez), while only 50 miles to the west it meets the Pacific Ocean. Prior to the opening of the Trans-peninsular Highway in 1973, only the hardiest and most adventurous travelers journeyed down the peninsula with four-wheel drive vehicles, or along its coastal edges by boat. Even now, much of this land's vast interior is inaccessible by road.

Europeans first set foot in this seemingly desolate land in 1533. Under the flag of Spain, Hernán Cortés set out to explore the Pacific in hopes of finding a passage across North America. At this time the peninsula was thought to be a long island, inhabited only by native peoples such as the Guaycura in the south and the Cochimi in the north. One with the land, these people had perfected the art of living in balance with their barren surroundings.

Dispatched by Cortés, Fortún Jiménez and his crew first reached La Paz Bay in the Gulf of California in late 1533. Shortly thereafter, Jiménez and many crewmembers were killed by the local Indians. Survivors, however, reported finding black pearls in the Bay. The discovery of these pearls, together with Spain's interest in colonizing the area, encouraged further exploratory trips to the peninsula.

Cortés himself traveled to Baja California, as did other famous explorers including Ulloa, Vizcaíno, Drake, Cavendish, and Cabrillo. Some of their lengthy journeys realized distances as far north as today's Oregon border in the United States.

History changed on the peninsula in 1697 with the establishment of the first mission at Loreto. After this intitial establishment, other tireless and optimistic missionary friars arrived looking to expand the territory of Spain through religion. These Jesuit *padres* founded 17 missions throughout Baja (Lower) California between 1697 and 1767. With the missions came the Spanish religion and culture, both of which still exist throughout the peninsula today.

From 1810 to 1821, Mexico fought for its independence from Spain, and in 1822 the peninsula became a part of the new nation of Mexico. Trouble was rekindled when the United States pre-cipitated the Mexican-American War commencing on May 11, 1846. In February, 1848, the Guadalupe Hidalgo Peace Treaty was signed, which allowed Mexico to retain Baja California.

Though much of the peninsula is uninhabited today, the Mexican government has recognized its beautiful treasures and has set aside several reserves and national parks. These range from the northernmost Constitución de 1857 National Park nestled in the Sierra de Juárez mountain range southeast of Tecate, to the southernmost Sierra de La Laguna National Park. In addition to these government-protected areas, one can find pristine wilderness throughout the peninsula.

It is these wild and beautiful treasures that are the subject and inspiration for this book. Join us to traverse these remote and nearly untouched areas throughout this long land of contrasts.

Along the Sea of Cortez

The terminus of California's notorious San Andreas fault is actually below the waters of the Sea of Cortez, also known as the Gulf of California. Millions of years ago, this fault line split Baja California from its mainland to the east. Plants native to Mexico found both on the peninsula and the adjacent mainland strongly indicate that these two land masses were once joined.

From the extensive tidal flats where the Colorado River joins the Sea of Cortez in the north, to the cape town of Cabo San Lucas in the south, this beautiful body of water has carved over 1,000 miles of coastline, still largely uninhabited and ripe for the explorer.

What painter catches each miniature island, surrounds it with water and color, only to change it all again tomorrow?

*F*orces from all directions create some of the most extensive tidal flats in the world. A combination of strong Sea of Cortez currents, the Colorado River delta, and a full moon can pull water distances up to two miles from the shoreline at high tide, attracting huge flocks of hungry shorebirds.

Near San Felipe, 20 miles south

Think not that the vast land is wasteland,
for countless creatures and succulents
call it "home."

*Candlesticks of yellow fire
reach toward the blue sky as
Brittlebush awakens from its drought
state to color the foothills of the
Sierra de San Felipe.*

Near San Felipe

*One eye sees a multitude of grounded
flowers hugging the desert floor for comfort,
yet the other sees the stars and galaxies
of the heavens . . . and the mind wonders
if they are one.*

*Wildflowers soften the desert
surface, which is sharply contrasted
by the soothing blue horizon
of the Sea of Cortez.*

Near Puertecitos

*Even on the most isolated shorelines of Baja California,
one is sure to come upon real Mexican fishing camps. A common way of life
for the locals, fishermen leave home for weeks at a time, traveling
in their boats — pangas — for miles along deserted coastline in their
search for a profitable catch.*

Shelter of the night life, Adam welcomes the nocturnal darkness protecting all with the bark of his arms.

Bay of the Spirits was most likely named by 17th- and 18th-century seafarers in the days of the Spanish conquistadors, who were probably struck by the eerie and abrupt changes from ocean swells to complete calm. Set deep into the coastline, the bay is often used as a resting and unloading place for local fishermen. The surrounding arroyos are colored with blue, purple, and gray rocks washed down from the mountains above. Back-lit with the evening light, the whiskers of the Senita — Old Man Cactus — glow. In its early stages of growth, Senita seeks protection from wind and animals, growing within the gnarls of this Adam's Tree. The beautiful white flower of the Senita opens at night to accommodate bat and insect pollinators. The Adam's Tree closely resembles an Ocotillo but has a short trunk before branching out. Both the Ocotillo and Adam's Tree quickly sprout green leaves after a rain.

Bahía de las Animas,
20 miles southeast of Bahía de los Angeles

*Dare I sculpt when nature's hand
has mastered such perfection?*

Near El Barril

*Alluvial fans from dry rivers provide hospitable sedimentation
for many of the native Baja California plants. A few of these river beds
are wet through the winter, creating fertile lagoons rich with the
minerals crucial to the survival of many plants and animals.*

The evening shadow cast by a lonely Cardón adds interest to the glow of the rich virgin soil and the sky's deep blue overhead. San Francisquito has long been a treasured destination of the seasoned bush pilot. Isolated from nearly all traffic, the grainy beaches and peaceful blue of the Sea of Cortez have lured many adventurous airborne travelers.

San Francisquito

*The compass guides me northward, where nature blesses me
with sea life . . . Hark! I sit in silence.*

Near Las Tres Virgenes,
northwest of Santa Rosalía

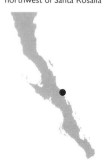

*These three prominent volcanic cones are important landmarks
for the traveler at sea, by land, and in the air. The paved highway leaves
the central town of San Ignacio and passes these mountains before
dropping down to the old copper mining town of Santa Rosalía. In 1885,
the Mexican government allowed a French company to mine the hills
to the north. Quiet coves and bays to the north, inaccessible by car, support
seal colonies and several species of sharks and whales, as well as cloud-filled
vistas lit with the rays of the western sun.*

Near Santa Rosalía, 10 miles southeast

Tidal flats create pools that teem with saltwater organisms, some too small to see. Moments before darkness, the vast sky seems to reflect the ripples of the sleepy Sea of Cortez.

*A descending sun acknowledges the day's finale
and wishes comfort to those who sleep.*

Cabo San Lucas

*O*ften referred to by the locals as Land's End, this once-sleepy
fishing village is now a bustling resort town. A temperate climate, sandy
beaches, and the best sport fishing in the world are its claim to fame. Avid
fishermen in search of Marlin, tuna, and Rooster Fish scan the skies for
flocks of Magnificent Frigatebirds. These birds follow the huge schools of
small fish that precede a Marlin feeding frenzy. Though Cabo San Lucas'
streets are lined with hotels and restaurants, a sunset view of the last stretch
of land, which is finalized by a natural arch in the sea, is a calming
reminder of the wild beauty found throughout the peninsula.

Roaming the Interior Deserts & Canyons

Much of Baja California is in fact part of the vast Sonoran Desert, a desert which stretches into mainland Mexico and the United States. Elevations in the peninsula's arid interior range from sea level to over 4,000 feet, encompassing miles and miles of unspoiled desert wilderness. In areas such as the Desierto Central de Baja California, one can identify hundreds of species of native cacti. The vast El Vizcaino Biosphere Reserve is an isolated wedge of land that is flat yet beautiful in its unique way.

These deserts often give way to transition zones leading to the dramatic mountain regions. In these transition areas, moist mountainscape quickly gives way to dry desertscape. Canyons on occasion run with water, creating pools and streams that reveal jewels of lush plant and animal life. The life-giving canyons provide sustenance to the people inhabiting these areas, today as in the past.

Silhouetted pillars searching for the heavens anchor themselves in a trusting terrain.

*N*ovember and December
rains, coupled with intermittent
spring showers, determine the vigor
of the spring bloom in the desert.
The vibrant red flowers of the
Hummingbird Flower attract
chuparosas—hummingbirds—
such as Anna's and Costa's. Many
varieties of Cholla cacti grow on
the desert floor, providing nesting
habitat for Cactus Wrens and
food for Mule Deer.

Near La Ventana,
65 miles southeast of Mexicali

... and the rocks whispered to the sun above and the blue palms below, "Mark me, but only for an instant," as an angel fish becomes marooned in a shallow canyon.

Indians frequented the canyon pathways which led from their higher-altitude summer camps down to Laguna Salada, a dry lake bed. Laguna Salada fills and drains with the rains and occasional tidal activity of the nearby delta, which joins the Colorado River and the Sea of Cortez. Rain collects deep below the surface in the canyon crevices, providing perfect conditions for the endemic Mexican Blue Palm — Palma Ceniza — and stately California Fan Palm.

Cañon el Tajo, 35 miles southwest of Mexicali

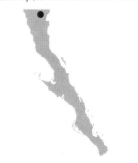

The beauty of the spiny-pronged cacti beckons one precariously nearer.

*A*long the eastern escarpment of the Sierra de Juárez, canyons drop abruptly to the desert below. Pines quickly give way to prickly cactus as elevations drop from 5,000 feet to below sea level in only a few miles.

Cañon de Guadalupe,
40 miles southwest of Mexicali

From the crevice of granite
oozes water that gives birth to life anew.

*Eight thousand feet below the
alpine vegetation of Picacho del
Diablo, spring runoff from the
snow-clad peaks spills into the dry
desert. Spiny Rushes store drops of
this precious moisture in their
roots, in hopes of surviving
the coming summer.*

Cañon del Diablo, 30 miles west of San Felipe

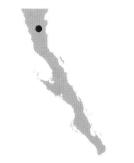

Sandle-footed, I walk the foothills and marvel at the many forms of nothingness ... of everything ...

Seemingly endless gardens of cacti complement the surrounding hills that lead away from the coast and into this most unique and diverse treasure of desert flora found anywhere in the world. Desert Agave was used by Indians for healing burns and wounds, and Barrel Cactus provided an emergency source of water. The Agave produces a large asparagus-looking stalk that is over five feet tall, which only once blooms into vibrant clusters of yellow flowers.

Near El Rosario, 60 miles east

$\mathcal{H}$ighway 1 is the only paved road that threads the entire length of the peninsula. The road jogs east from El Rosario and then heads south through Desierto Central de Baja California, a beautiful preserve where botanists have found many native and unique desert plants. Cataviña's desert garden is populated by hundreds of remarkably adaptable drought-tolerant plants. Cholla, Ocotillo, Elephant Trees, Boojum Trees, and Cardón rise into the vast skies. They provide beautiful silhouettes as days quickly blend into years in this timeless wilderness.

Cataviña

The Cirio, or Boojum Tree, received its name from the Spanish, who thought the tree resembled the wax candles used in their missions. This mid-peninsula tree is found nowhere else in the world except for a small colony across the Sea of Cortez in the mainland state of Sonora, near the town of Libertad. This colony suggests that the peninsula was part of the mainland prior to the land division caused by the San Andreas fault. Since it takes up to 40 years to grow three feet, some of the Boojum Trees that reach 80 feet are estimated to be more than 360 years old.

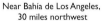
Near Bahía de Los Angeles,
30 miles northwest

$\mathcal{C}$ardón is the tallest cactus in the Sonoran Desert, reaching heights in excess of 60 feet. The sponge-like flesh between the cactus ribs holds water, expanding and contracting with rainfall and drought. Holes in the trunk are used by woodpeckers and owls, while hawks sometimes use the massive Cardón arms for nesting sites. Spines around the small cactus fruit shed easily when the fruit is ripe, allowing feeding access for birds. Often confused with Arizona's Saguaro Cactus, the Cardón is found only in Baja California and a select few areas of mainland Mexico. Cardón typically has much longer arms that branch closer to the base of the plant, compared to the shorter and higher arms of the Saguaro.

Near Bahía San Luis Gonzaga

Near Punta Abreojos, 35 miles northeast

*D*esierto de Vizcaíno, named after the Spanish navigator who
visited the area in 1596, is a vast and isolated desert region in the heart of
the peninsula. Fog, created when temperatures from land and ocean
clash, is often the only moisture this area receives in a year. A few
lonely roads traverse the area, offering four-wheel enthusiasts
a chance to see the outback.

Wet waters will their way along wide
arroyos and thirsty sands lap up their
moisture just as quickly.

*Y*ears of flash floods from the
Sierra Tinaja de Murillo have
created a desert wash as wide as
many major North American rivers.
The mesas above are the home of Los
Californios, the last of the Hispanic
mountain-dwelling cowboys who
still today have retained the old
ways of their Spanish forefathers. The
landscape surrounding this Palo
Blanco tree is marked by the sharp
contrasts of green, blue, brown, and
white. Los Californios use the trunks
of these trees to build the walls of
their mountain homes. Water from
the arroyos is trapped and carried
in hollowed palm logs to small
gardens and homes, sustaining their
unique and isolated lifestyle.

Rio San Carlos,
40 miles northwest of Santa Rosalía

San Ignacio

At the end of a long trip south through the dry and desolate Vizcaíno Desert, one suddenly comes upon the truest of desert oases, San Ignacio. Date palms and citrus trees, which were planted by the priests in 1728, are nestled in a wide arroyo. They surround the original mission which has since been reconstructed and is still standing. The Spanish influence is evident in the mission's architecture and front courtyard, which is still the focus of local life today.

*A grave marking has unearthed and earthed itself again,
burying a soul with volumes of one life.*

San Ignacio

*Missionaries, first led by Padre Juan María Salvatierra,
established 17 mission sites from 1697 to 1767. These European settlements
planted the foundation of many of today's lively peninsular communities.*

Trekking the *Sierras & Foothills*

Pools, streams, waterfalls, pine forests, and chaparral-covered mesas can be found in these mountainous islands in the desert. At the northern border of Baja California is the beginning of the Sierra de Juárez mountain range, dipping at San Matías Pass before rising again to the peninsula's highest point in the Sierra San Pedro Mártir range. In central Baja California, mesas slowly rise along the gulf before reaching the Sierra La Giganta range south of Loreto. Then just north of the southern tip, the peninsula makes one final stretch for the sky, peaking at 7,030 feet at Picacho de la Laguna. These mountain regions are all important veins of life that support a long history of Indians, missionaries, and modern settlements.

Two spoon-laid slabs of granite find comfort in one another's nearness.

Laguna Hanson,
40 miles southeast of La Rumorosa

*T*he Sierra de Juárez mountain range is the beginning
of the "backbone" of northern Baja California. Nestled among pine trees
and granite boulders, the dry lake of Laguna Hanson fills and drains with
the seasons. The landscape hints of the desert below and the mountains
above, from harsh, windblown exfoliating granite to the colder-growing
Mexican Piñon Pines and the Single-Needle Piñons.

Light as a winged Monarch, I perch among the blossoms connecting man to flora and fauna.

*T*his park boasts the highest point in Baja California, Picacho del Diablo, at 10,154 feet. Pericome, a late-season bloomer, is often found along mountain roads and provides ideal camouflage for this Monarch butterfly. The Spaniards named this brightly flowered plant Yerba de Chivato — herb of the goat — due to its odor.

San Pedro Mártir National Park

Near Valle de Trinidad

In the peninsula's beautiful transition zones between mountains and coast, extensive foothills are covered by chaparral. Plants in these areas, such as Yucca, usually range in height from three to 13 feet. Chaparral plants are often able to withstand fires by regenerating through fire-resistant seeds or resprouting from stumps.

Oh mountains . . . how fashionably you dress yourself in monochromatic hues.

Mike's Sky Rancho,
25 miles southeast of Valle de Trinidad

Beautiful terraces of mountains and hills fade into the foggy horizon of the distant Pacific. This rustic mountain resort, with its striking vistas, has long been a favorite of support crews of off-road racers, who compete to be the first to arrive in La Paz after battling 1,000 miles of relentless terrain.

*B*elow the 9,000-foot
mountain range of the Sierra
San Pedro Mártir, snowmelt and
rainfall is quickly channeled through
canyons destined for the desert floor.
Vegetation, such as this Willow grove,
intercepts the water for its own use,
quickly depriving the plants below
of this fresh water source.

Cañon del Diablo

Near Meling Ranch, 20 miles east

*A lone Jeffrey Pine separates the colors of the sky
before fading into pitch dark, the wake-up call of the astronomer. In 1976,
Universidad de Mexico took advantage of the extraordinarily clear skies
atop the mountains of the Sierra San Pedro Mártir, and built three
astronomical observatories. Though it is one of the wider sections of
the peninsula, one can see both the Pacific Ocean and the Sea of
Cortez from this 9,000-foot vantage point.*

Coastal mountains, 25 miles
northwest of Bahía San Luis Gonzaga

*R*ugged cerros—rocky mountains—and mesas seem lifeless from
offshore; however, this territory is home to the Desert Bighorn Sheep. An
occasional mountain spring will provide the water necessary to keep
this secretive and sure-footed animal alive.

*O*n the western slopes of the
*Sierra de La Laguna mountains,
water is far more abundant than in
the rest of the peninsula. Sparks of
yellow flowers from a native tree add
a bouquet of color to an area spotted
with ranchos, where beef is raised
for the local communities. The
availability of water has enabled
the development of towns and
agriculture in areas such as
Todos Santos and Santiago.*

Los Pozos, 15 miles north of Cabo San Lucas

Exploring the Islands & Pacific Ocean

Teeming with marine life,
the Pacific Ocean and the
islands around the peninsula
are rich and isolated environs.
Islands in both the Pacific and
the Sea of Cortez are perfect
breeding grounds for many
animal and bird species,
such as whales, elephant seals,
terns, and sea lions.
The coastal Pacific offers a
temperate climate in the
northern and southern regions,
while its central shoreline
is harsh and dry.

Marine life is abundant on the Pacific Ocean's continental shelf. Near this bay's southern point — La Bufadora — cool currents from the north mesh with the temperate waters of the south. This creates an underwater world that bustles with sea life, making it well-known in scuba diving circles.

Bahía de Todos Santos, Ensenada

A prelude to tomorrow awaits.

Santa Rosalillita, 40 miles
north of Guerrero Negro

The tranquil beaches north and south of this sleepy Mexican village have been discovered not only by a large seal colony, but also by the more adventuresome surfers of Alta — upper — California. Uninterrupted beauty and a perfect climate make this nook hard to leave for seals and surfers alike.

Lead me to learn, mother, for I have a life of exploring to do.

Isla Lobos, Islas Encantadas,
15 miles southeast of Puertecitos

$\mathcal{H}$arbor Seals and Sea Lions bask in the evening sun,
taking full advantage of their vast private playground
off the remote Baja California shore.

Crafty mariners anchoring themselves at sunset.

Near Isla Encantada,
20 miles southeast of Puertecitos

𝓔very April the string of "enchanted islands" in the northern gulf is the home and nesting ground for thousands of Heermann's Gulls, Yellow-footed Gulls, and Brown Pelicans. An imaginary five-foot radius is all that separates one nest from the next, almost perfectly patterned across these otherwise quiet desert islands.

Scammon's Lagoon,
10 miles south of Guerrero Negro

The warm, shallow, and protected waters of Scammon's Lagoon are the perfect winter courting and breeding grounds for the California Gray Whale. Each year approximately 1,500 new calves are born in these lagoons. Their 3,800-mile annual migration from the coasts of Alaska is the longest of any mammal. The stillness of the morning is often broken by the breathing, spouting, and playing of these 30-ton gentle gaints, which can often be heard for up to five miles across the perfectly calm waters.

Somewhere between the Heavens and Earth God created a puzzle
from patches of clouds for each of us to assemble.

La Bocana

*Thirty-five miles southwest of the paved road, through the Vizcaíno
Desert, the Pacific fishing villages of Punta Abreojos and La Bocana give
life to an otherwise desolate stretch of pristine beach. The most adventurous
of los norteamericanos have made the long journey south to surf these waters.
In March and April, California Gray Whales — Ballena Gris — which
winter in the nearby San Ignacio Bay, make their way north to their
summer home in the waters off the coast of Alaska. Dozens of these
whales may be seen in a day as they follow the continental
shelf to their northern destination.*

A power greater than that within us plants a hand among the stones and splays its fingers as if to grasp the universe.

This Organ Pipe Cactus — Pitaya Dulce — flanks the distinct horizon and the imaginary line where the Pacific Ocean finally meets the Sea of Cortez. The Indians cherished the sweet fruit of this cactus. The tennis ball-sized prize was retrieved with a hook attached to the end of a dried Cardón cactus rib. Even today, the fruit is harvested in late summer and fall, and is eaten and used to make fresh tropical drinks.

Faro Viejo, near Cabo San Lucas

Near Todos Santos, 20 miles south

This Cardón forest is the perfect habitat for nesting and hunting Osprey. The thick vegetation is home to a never-ending supply of snakes and rodents, while the sea provides an equally abundant supply of fish for the diverse diet of these skilled hunters.

About the *Authors*

Raised in Southern California's Imperial Valley on the United States–Mexico border, **James Kuhn** has spent parts of the past three decades traveling and exploring the most remote of Baja California's varied regions.

As he worked on the family farm during his teens, Jim often had the opportunity to gaze on Mt. Signal, a singular peak that prominently straddles the border in the Imperial Valley. This mountain seemed to signal to Jim to "come see the other side."

Jim's first trips into the peninsula's remote interior during the 1970's were to assist the mechanical crews for off-road races. Even then he was able to appreciate the quiet beauty and wild promise of this unique land. For the next two decades, he took countless trips of varying lengths to areas that have only been visited by the most adventurous. Jeep and bushpilot trips, hiking, mountain biking, and kayaking provided the means to reach ever more remote and beautiful areas. During these adventures, Jim's true love for the peninsula, its people, and places grew strong.

Jim has furthered his explorations by learning much about Baja California's natural history, and has applied a second love, photography, to his travels. In addition to four photo exhibits, Jim's work has been published in books, on magazine covers, and his own self-published photographic *Guide to the Birds of the Imperial Valley.*

By capturing the area's natural treasures on film and combining them with his knowledge of the region, Jim hopes to ignite others' enthusiasm for this remote and beautiful land of contrasts.

Dr. Vreneli Kuhn Wilson spent forty years in the Imperial Valley, an agricultural area along the California and Mexico border. From elementary grades on, she found a kinship with words that mirrored her inner feelings.

Vreneli's interests are in sharing the love of learning, reading, and writing with young minds. She began her teaching career at Seeley and McCabe

Elementary, two small country schools outside of El Centro, California.

Throughout the years Vreneli has written curricula, taught university reading courses, written instructional manuals, and given training seminars to teachers, aides, and parents. She has worked for Houghton–Mifflin and The Economy Publishing Companies. Vreneli participated on several boards, serving as president of the Cardiff–by–the–Sea Chamber of Commerce for two years. She has also been featured in a documentary dealing with stress-related topics produced by Five Star Productions of Los Angeles, California.

Vreneli received her doctorate from Northern Arizona University, in Flagstaff, Arizona. There she studied theories and methods of teaching reading.

Today Vreneli lives in San Diego, California. She owns a reading clinic in Cardiff–by–the–Sea, California, where she continues to pass on her love of reading, learning and writing.

Selected *Bibliography* and *Additional* *Reading*

Crosby, Harry W., 1994. *Antigua California: Mission and Colony on the Peninsular Frontier, 1697–1768*. University of New Mexico Press, Albuquerque, New Mexico.

Crosby, Harry W., 1981. *Last of the Californios*. Copley Books, La Jolla, California.

Crosby, Harry W., 1984. *The Cave Paintings of Baja California*. Copley Books, La Jolla, California.

Dickey, Kathleen Johnson. 1983. *A Natural History Guide to Baja California*. Chula Vista, California.

Kira, Gene. 1997. *King of the Moon: A Novel of Baja California*. Apples and Oranges Publishers, Valley Center, California.

Krutch, John Wood. 1986. *The Forgotten Peninsula: A Naturalist in Baja California*. University of Arizona Press, Tucson, Arizona.

Mackintosh, Graham. 1988. *Into a Desert Place: A 3,000 Mile Walk Around the Coast of Baja California*. Unwin Hyman Limited, London, England.

McNally, Robert. 1981. *So Remorseless a Havoc: Of Dolphins, Whales and Men*. Little, Brown & Co., Ltd., Boston, Massachusetts.

Morrison, Wilbur H., 1990. *The Adventure Guide to Baja California*. Hunter Publishing, Inc.

Roberts, Norman C., 1989. *Baja California Plant Field Guide*. Natural History Publishing Co., La Jolla, California.

Romano-Lax, Andromeda. 1993. *Sea Kayaking in Baja*. Wilderness Press, Berkeley, California.

Senterfitt, Arnold D., 1987. *Airports of Baja California and Northwest Mexico*. Baja Bush Pilots, Vista, California.

Wilbur, Sanford R., 1987. *Birds of Baja California*. University of California Press, Berkeley, California.

Wong, Bonnie. 1988. *Bicycling Baja*. Sunbelt Publications, San Diego, California.

Zwinger, Ann. 1983. *A Desert Country Near the Sea*. Harper and Row, Pub., New York.

Acknowledgments

Certainly one of the greatest gifts for which I am thankful is having Baja California literally in my backyard. However, the places and feelings documented in this book would not have near the meaning without the leadership, friendship and companionship of a handful of people.

A special thanks to Norman Roberts for the use of his detailed maps at the beginning of the book, as well as for his review of the text. I am also grateful to Harry Crosby for reviewing the historical aspects of the text and for his encouraging words about becoming an author. To Betsy Knaak and Karen Hollingsworth, I am indebted for their review of the book style and layout and for their support in general of all my projects.

For my interest in photography I am specifically grateful to my brother, John Kuhn, who bought me my first "real" camera, and who supported and encouraged me tirelessly as I struggled through the initial stages of trying to create and compose a photograph.

My true interest in the outback of the peninsula was motivated by long-time family friend and outdoor adventurer, Jack Strobel. When I contemplated a single–vehicle attempt of "Baja's roughest road" from San Felipe to Gonzaga Bay, Jack cautiously instructed me on the difficulties, yet with a glimmer in his eye, was hopeful I would try it.

The first flight down the peninsula was, unbeknownst to me, only one of many to follow. I thank Bill McConnell for his calm and collected piloting skills, and best of all for his love of Baja California's peaceful presence.

I am deeply indebted to my close friends and traveling companions. I thank Craig Hoagland who enthusiastically shared with me his love of kayaking. Together we have kayaked both sides of the peninsula and attempted to hike to its highest point. I also thank Jay Petersen for accepting the challenge of "Baja's roughest road" and providing the necessary comic relief along the way. I thank Ross Koda for several successful fishing outings at the Cape and at La Bocana, and for his inspiring comments that there is more to a photograph than sunsets.

Having spent the most miles on the peninsula with me, sharing love and friendship, I thank my wife Heidi. Willingly she gave hours of her time to this project in support, editing, ideas, feedback, reason, and reassurance.